SUCCESS

More Than Your Resume?

CHARLES LEE and
ROBERT FRANK

ISBN: 0692234306
ISBN-13: 978-0692234303

ABOUT THIS SERIES

VeriTalks were created to cultivate ongoing conversations seeded by live Veritas Forum events.

Each VeriTalk includes both the original talk and audience Q&A to draw you more intimately into the conversation. Discussion questions—both personal and intellectual—are incorporated into the talk to deepen your engagement with the material, ideally in the company of friends. The questions are repeated at the end of the book for easy reference.

We hope this series will catalyze your exploration of True Life.

CONTENTS

ACKNOWLEDGMENTS

This talk was originally presented at The Veritas Forum at Cornell University in 2013 under the title, "You Are NOT Your Resume."

Many thanks to the students, faculty and campus organizations who helped create this event.

TWO VIEWS OF SUCCESSFUL LIVING

PROFESSOR CHARLES LEE: A CHRISTIAN VIEW

I'M REALLY HAPPY TO BE HERE. I know everybody starts by saying that, but in my case I have some credentials to back it up. I got my graduate degrees here, spending four years at Cornell, then I went away for six years, then came back for eight years. I was a faculty member here and my wife I have two kids here. We have four degrees among the four of us from Cornell. And we've lived here longer than we've lived anywhere: 12 years. We're currently on the West Coast, but we love Cornell.

I'm not only happy, I'm also grateful to be here. On our way here we took a bit of a detour, so I flew east on Thursday and my first stop was Boston. I was supposed to give a research seminar yesterday at Boston University. I arrived about the same time as Obama, but he left before I did. And when I woke up on Friday morning the whole city was on lockdown; my hotel was a couple of blocks from where the original explosions were. Basically, instead of having a research seminar, all 15 campuses were closed and I had a lot of time to sit in my hotel room and think about the world we live in. And a lot of that flavors what I'm going to share with you today.[*]

Is success a good thing? Let me just start by asking a question. This is way too big a group to cold call, but what do you think of success? Is success a good thing? How many of you *don't* want to be successful? Just put up your hand. You know, I think most people think of success as a good thing. But what about being a successful liar, a successful thief? What about being a successful terrorist? Not so good, right?

When we think about success, we're defining it in terms of

---

[*] Prof. Lee is referring to the events surrounding the Boston Marathon bombing of April 15, 2013.

a goal. We define success as the attainment of some sort of goal, and the real question is: *Is your goal any good?* The success of a knife is to cut, because it was designed to cut. The success of a race horse is to run, because it was bred to run. So what does success look like for a human being?

That depends on what you think a human being is. In order to ask these questions, you need some sort of a worldview, some sort of coherent, metaphysical commitment to something. It's like having an answer to the questions that the security guard will ask you when he finds you in the middle of the night: *Who are you? What are you doing here? Where are you going?*

Success and worldview. And no matter how you address the question of success or the pursuit of happiness – in some sense, we all have some intuitive response – that cogent worldview is going to affect how you live.

In fact, as a Christian, I think there is a lot more to life than just trying to be successful at work. I'm sure Professor Frank would agree with that because I've read some of the things he has written and I've known him as a friend for many years.

Even in the work setting, how we live out our lives makes a huge difference in the success that we experience, at least in terms of meaning and purpose. In fact, I think it's self-evident that how we choose to live our lives cannot be separated from what we believe in.

Day-to-day lives are shaped by what we believe in. Certainly that has been true in my own life and career, decisions, choices. So let me just tell you a little bit about myself, at least how I ended up being a Christian.

My Christian worldview. I wasn't born a Christian. I grew up in Taiwan and when I was nine years old, my parents immigrated to Canada. I grew up in Southern Ontario. My mom became a Christian first; my father was a very articulate atheist.

So I grew up…'religiously confused' is the right term. And I felt like God never introduced himself to me. When I got to college, God and I were sort of in a truce. I couldn't say there was no God, but at the same time, I felt like I had no reason to really know him. I felt that if you wanted me to worship him and I didn't worship him and he sent me someplace unpleasant, then he wouldn't be much of a God worth worshipping anyway.

So growing up in North America, there are lots of things that seemed more relevant like photography, fly-fishing, girls, you know, stuff. It didn't really occur to me to think too much about whether God existed until the end of my college life. At that point, several things in my life caused me to think again. One of them was that my father contracted cancer. And the other is that I had a few failed romances. That's the nicest way of putting it: I had a few set backs in my relational exploits. Usually it's the other person's fault, of course, but somewhere along the way I discovered I don't have control over the most important things in my life, including my feelings, my emotions, my sense of rage or jealousy or lust – many things.

And I started to wonder again whether God really exists, and that question hung there for a while, until the fall of 1982. I'd just graduated. My father, who had been quite sick, became a Christian. And my parents invited me to a Christian camp. I would not have gone except for the fact that I had already made arrangements to take a week off and all of my friends wimped out. So I had a whole week off; I had no choice. And the place they chose for the retreat was Finland Falls, Ontario, which is a great fishing place. So I ended up going. And the fishing was really lousy and I ended up spending more time in Bible study than I thought I was going to.

To keep the story short, basically, I remember the first night they were doing Bible study. And one passage really hit me, a passage that says, "All have sinned and fall short of the glory of God." I had never actually paid a whole lot of attention to the Bible, but somehow this "all have sinned" made me think again and say, "Well, if 'all' means everyone, I'm a proper subset of that. So I have sinned." And for the first time in my life, something resonated with me on that.

And so, that was the beginning of that week, and somewhere along the way, someone asked me if I would want to receive Jesus into my life. No one had ever asked me that. At that moment, I suddenly realized: If God is knowable, that was the thing I wanted to know more than anything else. So this guy was asking, "Would you raise your hand?" I was scared to death. I don't know why I was scared to death, but I raised my little hand.

That precipitated a series of changes and two feelings in particular. One was an experience of inexpressible joy. I was extremely happy. I wanted to hug people when I went down the street. The other was some sort of recognition or dawning or an awareness. I remember staying up all night realizing I screwed up a lot in my life. There were a lot of things I couldn't remember that I'd screwed up – and they all came pouring back at me. And I could actually understand this book – the Bible – and I started reading it. Before that, I could never go more than a sentence or two; I'd thought it was silly. So that led to a lot of changes, including my decision to enroll in a PhD, to become a teacher, to apply to Cornell, and then, also my career. I don't have much time today to tell you, but eventually leading me to come and be here today.

Why is success elusive? And I guess I would say that here's the crux of it: you know we all want to live well. We all want to be happy, generally successful, but to do that, you have to ask yourself: *Why is it so elusive in this human journey?* What is the human dilemma that makes happiness and success such a challenge?

In fact, let me throw this out. This is one we're not going to disagree on at all: there is no real search for happiness that can be had apart from the search for virtue, for goodness.

This truth is taught to us through much of our religious as well as cultural heritage, including the Greek stoics. If you think that you can find happiness apart from looking for what goodness means or virtue means, you will find yourself in a very strange corner in which you have neither.

Why is it so hard to be good? But the question is: *Why is it so hard to be good?* And for me, being a Christian, I find a very satisfying response in the Bible. That we who were built as God-centered creatures became through certain processes – we call it "falling" – self-centered creatures. And the self-centered creature is going to find a lot of problems. Music doesn't quite play the way it should play in our lives.

David Foster Wallace has written a little book called, *This Is Water*. You can find it on YouTube, because this whole book is basically a transcript of his 2005 commencement address to Kenyon College. He has some really cool things to say. Let me just read to you this little passage (I recommend the whole book to you in its entirety):

> *In the day-to-day trenches of adult life, there is actually no such thing as atheism. There is no such thing as not worshipping. Everybody worships. The only choice we get is what to worship.*

> *And an outstanding reason for choosing some sort of God or spiritual-type thing to worship – be it Jesus Christ or Allah, be it Yahweh or the Wiccan mother-goddess or the Four Noble Truths or some infrangible set of ethical principles – is that pretty much anything else you worship will eat you alive.*

If you worship money and things – if they are where you tap real meaning in life – then you will never have enough. Never feel you have enough. It's the truth.

Worship your own body and beauty and sexual allure and you will always feel ugly, and when time and age start showing, you will die a million deaths before they finally plant you.

On one level, we all know this stuff already – it's been codified as myths, proverbs, clichés, bromides, epigrams, parables: the skeleton of every great story. The trick is keeping the truth up-front in daily consciousness.

Worship power – you will feel weak and afraid, and you will need ever more power over others to keep the fear at bay.

Worship your intellect, being seen as smart – you will end up feeling stupid, a fraud, always on the verge of being found out. And so on.

Look, the insidious thing about these forms of worship is not that they're evil or sinful; it is that they are unconscious. They are default-settings.

There was a time when a university education could not be separated from matters of faith and morality. I understand why there is more separation now but I think maybe the pendulum has swung around too much. We spend all our time in universities siloed, talking about technical knowledge, sectoral knowledge. We privatize faith. And in the aftermath of this Boston event, we need to ask ourselves: *Does the world really need more smart people or more good people?*

QUESTIONS FOR DISCUSSION

- *Can you sketch your basic worldview using the "security guard" questions: Who are you? Why are you here? Where are you going?*

- *How would you define success right now? Can you trace how your worldview shapes your particular vision of success?*

- *Professor Lee emphasizes the importance of virtue in human happiness. In your experience, how are the two related? Have you experienced one without the other?*

- *Given the quotation from David Foster Wallace, what are your "default settings"? Have you experienced – or seen others – being "eaten alive" by what they worship?*

- *How do you respond to Professor Lee's critique of privatized faith and a siloed university? What other models are there for education and morality?*

? For an audience question related to this topic, see page 38 *(Should morality be integrated into our university system?).*

SUCCESS

ROBERT FRANK: A DARWINIAN VIEW

I CAN'T SAY I'M GLAD TO BE BACK IN ITHACA because I've been in Ithaca for 42 years. I started teaching here in 1972 and I used to feel surprised to be able to say, "Since before you were born," but now I can say, "Since before your parents were born, I've been teaching at Cornell."

I got a note from a colleague today saying she'd seen a poster advertising this event in Golden Smith Hall. And she said, "What is this event about?" There were two big head shots of Charles and me, and across his face was in big red letters "Christian" and across my face it was "Atheist." Apparently the event was framed as a violent clash between two incredibly diametrically opposed ways of thinking about the world.

But from my knowledge of Charles and conversations with him over the years, I think what it'll really be more about is how people who view the world so differently can come to embrace such a similar essential view of how the world works and what's required for a life of harmony and contentment.

My Darwinian worldview. I was baptized as an Episcopalian and confirmed in that faith. I gradually drifted away. There is a lot of contingency in life. Maybe the people I hung out with were non-believers. (The trend in support for same-sex marriage has been sharply rising, and I think that's an example of the extent to which what people believe depends so strongly on what people around them that they care about and respect believe. When one more person shifts his opinion from View A to View B, that makes that seem a more normal view.)

There are all sorts of things people can believe. They sound strange to outsiders. My wife and I enjoyed the Book of Mormon. If you read the Book of Mormon literally, it sounds awfully strange to my ear, but if you imagine somebody from another planet reading the Bible, it would surely sound strange to his ear, too. So what we believe – all of us – is probably strange from a certain perspective.

But I have to make sense of the world as someone who doesn't believe that it's all being directed by a higher force, and so my intellectual framework is the one left to us by Charles Darwin. He, in my opinion, among mortal men, said the most informative things about how we got here and what the whole enterprise is about.

And it's a pretty simple scheme for him. In Darwin's view, individuals evolved by natural selection. The ones that were more likely to leave copies of their DNA to the next generation became more frequent and mutations were selected because they helped individual organisms. The purpose of the individual? To leave copies of your stuff into the next round. There's nothing very noble sounding about that.

And indeed, there is a lot of brutality in evolution. If you look at the behavior of lions, the lion who becomes the alpha male in a pride after defeating the incumbent alpha male, the very first thing he does is kill the cubs sired by the previous alpha male. He goes around and brutally shakes them and murders them. The reason he does that is a simple Darwinian one. It's that when the mothers of those cubs no longer have cubs to care for, they come into fertility cycle again more quickly, and so he gets to leave more copies of his genes behind in the next generation as a consequence of having done that.

Success does not equal goodness. So I think the impression people have when they think about Darwinism is that it's an utterly brutal framework for thinking about why organisms do what they do. It certainly does help explain a lot of the brutality that we see in the world, even among our species, but it's more than that. It's not the Spenserian social Darwinism.

It's not the survival of the fittest, "Nature, red in tooth and claw." It's not that. I think the big mistake when people think about the Darwinian framework is to think that because it survives, therefore it's good. One of Darwin's key insights was that many things survive because they help individuals survive and reproduce – that's why the traits are selected – but those same traits create general misery for the larger group the individuals belong to.

A nice example that captures that idea is the difference in size between the male and the female in most vertebrate species, but in particular some species like the elephant seal. The bull elephant seal is 21-23 feet long, he's 6,500 pounds. He weighs as much as a Lincoln Navigator. The female in that species weighs only 800 pounds. Why is the male so much bigger? Because it's a polygenous species, Darwin observed. The males take more than one mate if they can. The "if they can" qualifier is important. If some males take more than one mate, then some don't get any mates at all, and then you don't leave your stuff in the next round. So that's priority number one. How do you get a mate? You fight with other males to get a mate. So there was a mutation that made a bull bigger, he was more likely to win fights, so he had a harem of 50 cows all carrying the genes for that larger body size.

And it's a horrible thing for the bull elephant seals to weigh 6,500 pounds: they have to eat prodigious quantities; they're much more likely to be caught by sharks as they swim in the water because they're so fat and unmaneuverable; the arthritis they get at a young age is a consequence of that weight. If they could all sign an agreement and all reduce their body weight by two-thirds, they would have a compelling reason to do that. But that's not what evolution does. It doesn't work by agreement in animal species. It's just whatever works. That's what survives and gets reproduced into the next round.

Where humans part from that pattern is that we actually have the means – we have the cognitive ability, the emotional capacity and the communication skills – to try and solve these bitter conflicts that arise between the interests of the individual and the interests of the group.

Evolution of trustworthiness. So let me try to describe for you one simple dilemma that comes up in human society. Imagine that you're the owner of a small business, maybe it's Gimme Coffee, and you've got lines coming out the door. And you're established here. You know it'd work in a city 250 miles away – the market conditions are exactly right – but you can't manage it yourself, and you know that if you hire someone else to manage it, then you'll be at the mercy of that person. You won't be able to monitor the person's behavior well enough to prevent him or her from cheating you, and since he can't be punished for cheating, why wouldn't he cheat? What would be the motive if he were an atheist? Why shouldn't he cheat?

Well, if that's what you think all the people that you might hire would do (and that's what our model as economists encourages you to believe: *Homo economicus* does not vote, he does not give to charity, he does not do anything except what is in his own narrow interests), if that's what you think people are really all about, you can't start that venture, because if you do start it, you'll be ripped off.

But maybe that's not what the world is about. Maybe there *are* people you could find whom you could trust to manage your business honestly. How would you find them?

Here's a thought experiment I want to ask you to think about. You've gone to a very crowded event, and you have an envelope in your coat pocket with $10,000 dollars in cash in it. You were planning on buying a used car the next day and the owner wanted cash. You get home, you're hanging up your coat, and you notice the envelope is not in your pocket, and then you have that sinking feeling you heard that flap sound when you were putting your coat on and the envelope fell on the floor as you were leaving.

You will in effect be in a position to ask yourself: *Would someone like my employee John return it to me? I wouldn't know he found it. I would have no way to punish him if he didn't return it.* But you would have an opinion, if you're like most people. And if you're the boss of an employee that's worked for you for a couple years, you would have an opinion, in general, a pretty firm one, of whether he would or he wouldn't.

And those opinions, as we know from laboratory research, are surprisingly accurate about people. So if you want to get promoted, you want your boss to believe you would be someone who would return his envelope full of cash, if he thought about it in those terms. How can you get him to believe that?

Success in business. Groucho Marx said the secret to success in business is to have a reputation for honesty and fair dealing, and if you can fake that, you've really got it made!

"So, yeah. I'll try to appear honest," you may say. That's what the opportunist's goal is. But we're much better judges of character (for complicated Darwinian reasons). The reason you're honest is not because you make a rational calculation that it would good to be honest or rational to be honest. It's because you feel a duty to be honest, because you would feel empathy for the person who would suffer the injury if you cheated that person.

Those emotions which drive moral decisions in those contexts are like signs on your face. If you know someone well, you know what their emotional makeup is. And when you ask people, "Why were you so sure about that person? Why would he return your money?" the answer is, "I know him well enough to know that it just wouldn't compute for him to think about keeping my cash."

And that's what you want your boss to think about you when the time comes to be promoted. How can you get him to think that? It's very simple. Just be that kind of person. If you're not that kind of person, word of that will leak out one way or another. It will not necessarily be because you've been caught doing something, but because there will be some lack of inner peace that you experience or just something different about you that will make people not quite comfortable trusting you.

Evolution and virtue. What's different about the human species compared with all the other animal species is the extent to which we have been able to reap the advantages of economies of large scale production. We can divide tasks up. We can specialize. We can have lots of people doing different things. And put it all together in complex ways. That requires an enormous amount of cooperation and trust to achieve that. And that requires people you believe wouldn't cheat you if they had a chance to do it when nobody would catch them.

So do you want to be successful? I think most people do want to be successful. I don't think that's a bad thing, to want to be successful. But if you want to be successful, the steps that will lead you there with the greatest reliability are not the steps that somebody who wanted only to be successful would take.

The Buddhist way is instructive here. You get from point A to point B by maybe heading off in an oblique direction, on one side or the other, and you get there sooner rather than if you tried to plow ahead straight forward. So we'll have time to try to flesh that out as the program goes along. In the end, I think Charles and I come down to a pretty similar point of view on this.

SUCCESS

• *According to a Darwinian understanding, what makes humans unique? How does that square with your experience of being human?*

• *What are the elements of success, in Professor Frank's view?*

• *Professor Frank says that succeeding in being trusted is very simple:* "Just be that kind of person. If you're not that kind of person...there will be something different about you that will make people not quite comfortable trusting you." *What is your experience in "just being that kind of person"? Where do you think that "something different" comes from?*

• *How are virtue and success related from a Darwinian point of view? How does that compare with Professor Lee's approach or your own answer on page 8?*

• *Professor Frank implies that emotions drive moral decisions. How do you respond to that suggestion? How do you generate unaffected empathetic emotions?*

? For audience questions related to this topic, see page 35 (*As an atheist, how do I deal with the emptiness I feel in pursuing virtue as a means to harmony for the group?*), page 37 (*By what metric do you measure virtue?*), and page 43 (*Why do we see altruism in the human species but not in others?*).

DISCUSSION: CHARACTER, HAPPINESS AND MONEY

AIMING FOR CHARACTER?

Moderator Andrew Chignell: Can I follow up on the point you were just making? Because it relates to the agreement, but what also might be an underlying disagreement.

You both agree about the importance of success, aiming for certain kinds of goods; you both mentioned virtue and character as one of the ways in which that might look or incarnate itself.

But it sounded to me at the end as though your picture – as it may have been influenced by the sort of Darwinian narrative that you told – may have instrumentalized virtue a little bit. So emotions are important: we can read one another's emotions and intentions pretty easily. If you want to succeed, if you want to get to that goal, it's important that others read you as trustworthy, as having that sort of character. So have that character.

And you might think, aiming for character isn't supposed to be something that's *instrumental* in that way. So I wonder what you say in response?

Prof. Frank: There is an oxymoronic quality to the argument. I'm free to concede that. Somebody was told by his therapist to be more spontaneous. So he went out determined to be more spontaneous. And you just know that's not going to work.

I published a book outlining these ideas and I got a number of angry letters saying, "You're not supposed to be virtuous because it will benefit you." And I was sorry people didn't get my attempt to be clear in the book that that's not the *reason* to be virtuous, but if it meant that others can detect you as virtuous and favor you as an employee or a partner in interactions that require trust, it might be helpful to know that.

Say you have children trying to decide what path to take and they say, "I can either be virtuous or I can be opportunistic. If I'm opportunistic I'll be rich and famous; if I'm virtuous I'll be a pauper." If that's not in fact the tradeoff that children face but it's their perception, then it strikes me it might be a good idea to tell them that being virtuous wouldn't necessarily be fatal to their dreams of being prosperous in the material world. And I'm quick to say that if you're *trying* to be trustworthy, and trying to affect the emotions that make you seem trustworthy, people will immediately detect that you're trying to be trustworthy and they'll say, "That's not the employee I want."

Prof. Chignell: So what would be the independent reasons to be virtuous if not these opportunistic ones?

Prof. Frank: The emotions that we are born with, that we have the capacity to express, in my way of thinking about the world, had to have evolved for prudential reasons.

We know from cross-cultural studies that when a twelve-month-old child sees another kid in the group fall down and get hurt and start crying, they don't seem concerned about that. They'll look up to see who's crying and what the fuss is about; once they've satisfied that curiosity, they go back to whatever they were doing. But then in every society around the world, at about eighteen months to two years, children begin to manifest a genuine concern and sympathy for the kid who got hurt. They will stop what they're doing, they'll wander over to the kid who's crying and put an arm out. It's a concern for the other.

Why did that evolve if it makes you do things that cost you money, makes you give to charity? That's the central Darwinian question. And my answer to it is: those are the kinds of people we want on our team, the kinds of people who don't think only of their own welfare but who also think of our welfare. That's how those emotions came to be forged in the first instance, in my view of things.

But does that make them any less noble? Does that mean if you have to incur a painful sacrifice in order to help someone, that it isn't painful for you? No. The noblest things we see in human behavior are motivated by those suites of emotions that I think were forged step-by-step by natural selection. To say they are "just instrumental" is to miss the beauty of them. They're not demeaned in anyway by the fact that they have an explanation.

Prof. Lee: I think if I read what Bob said, he's providing a justification for why people might want to do good. Apart from religious faith, why people might want to be good. I don't think that is as much of an anomaly to me. (Maybe that is to some economists: the fact that people would want to do good is particularly puzzling.)

What I have observed in life is not that people don't recognize the currency of trust and doing good. It's this human dilemma: here is a creature who recognizes what good is but finds it difficult always to live that way.

We once had a debate in our Christian fellowship: Are people born good? At the end, what we concluded is that the human being would be alright if he were all good. And he would be fine too if he were all bad. But here was this weird creature who recognizes when he sees good but has a hard time living it.

There's a Harvard professor, Robert Kohls, who wrote an interesting article called, "The Disparity Between Intellect and Character." He teaches an ethics class and one day a student came in to his office. She was from a working class family and had to work in the dorms to make ends meet. Some of her classmates lived in the dorms and not all of them were nice to her. Some were crude, some were rude. In particular, one fellow made repeated overtures, propositioned her. She came in crying to Professor Kohls saying, "This boy gets straight A's in your class. If we wrote an essay on morality, he would get straight A's and I would probably get C's. Why is it that someone who knows so much about what is right does not live that way? Why would he behave that way?" Professor Kohls goes on to reflect about this to say there is a distance between between moral reasoning – our capacity to distinguish right from wrong – and moral behavior.

This gap to me is a telling empirical observation about my own life, because I see it everyday. If you've ever been to subways in London, you see the sign: Mind the gap. I would say in your life, look carefully. Mind the gap. Because that will tell you something about the world in which we live and perhaps about a world which we don't see empirically but which may have existed in our consciousness, a world where that morality was the norm, which we don't see now in this world. Maybe we're homesick for where we came from, when we used to belong to God.

QUESTIONS FOR DISCUSSION

• *Compare Professor Frank's and Professor Lee's views of the origins of virtue. Are they compatible?*

• *Given both professors' comments and your own experience, list all of the reasons for being virtuous. Which do you find most compelling? To what extent do any of those reasons enable you to be virtuous?*

• *Professor Lee draws a distinction between why we might strive for virtue, and how well we do at achieving it. Reflect on what he says about "minding the gap" in your own life.*

? For an audience question related to this topic (*If we're being good because God is watching, aren't we really being good out of fear? Or is there something else?*), see page 36.

SUCCESS

PURSUING HAPPINESS?

Prof. Chignell: Let's turn to the topic of happiness more directly. We've talked a little bit about success and virtue and our theories of the origins of virtue and how it works and how it sometimes doesn't work and where the gaps are.

What about happiness? What constitutes happiness and how does that relate to success in business and in the academy?

Prof. Frank: It's become a popular topic in the social sciences. There's a large and growing literature on the determinants of life satisfaction and happiness. The big debate for many years has been whether income affects happiness in the conventional way.

The findings come in two forms. One is that when they study income vs. happiness within a country at any moment in time, the average happiness level of poor people is significantly lower than the average happiness level of rich people. There's enormous variation at every income level.

If you want to be happy, the most important thing for you to have done is to have had happy parents. You can't do anything about that now that you're here, so income may be the biggest lever that is available to pull. There are other important factors too, but rich people are on average much happier than poor people. If you were born to unhappy parents and you were rich, you're liable to be unhappy even though you're rich. You might be blissfully happy even if you're poor if you had a naturally buoyant temperament to begin with.

But when we look at happiness over time and across countries that relationship is much weaker. If you look at Japan, for example, between 1960 and 2000, the income level rose fourfold but happiness level stayed flat as a pancake during that whole period. People were much richer; why didn't they get happier? Everybody was getting richer over time. So if, as some assume, what matters most beyond a certain point is where I stand relative to other people I know, if you're at the bottom of your group, it's natural to answer the question, "Where do I stand" with "I must not be doing all that well."

Relative income seems to matter a lot. There are some new studies showing up that as societies get richer over time, there are increases in measured happiness levels there too. We know there are good things that happen when societies get richer. They invest more in safety; they invest more in environmental cleanup; they invest more in trying to discover cures for debilitating diseases.

So if you're in a society and there's a policy question: Should we try to take steps to make the country wealthier? Well, you should guard the environment in the process, but having a wealthier society does good things in ways I think we'd find are uncontroversial.

Prof. Chignell: How are we defining happiness here?

Prof. Frank: Good question. The main variable that is used by happiness researchers is self-reported happiness. They come round and ask you: "How happy are you?" You're either "Not happy," "Pretty happy" or "Very happy." There are some that are more behavioral in nature. And there are more reflective questions: "All things considered, how satisfied with your life these days do you feel?" You might be having a lot of negative feelings but all things considered I think my life's going okay.

All these measures seem to agree. If you ask somebody: "Is your friend happy?" the friend's evaluation tends to agree with the evaluation. Economists in general are skeptical of these measures, but they've been vetted carefully and they do seem to correspond to measures that seem like valid measures we ought to care about.

Prof. Chignell: How would you define happiness?

Prof. Lee: I think in general, when we think about happiness, we think about well-being and contentment and the absence of the things you don't want: anxiety, worries, sense of insecurity.

I want to refer you to one passage in the Judeo-Christian narrative that's very telling to me. Even if you don't have a Judeo-Christian background, you know the story about Adam and Eve eating the forbidden fruit. What happened next, to me, is very telling. Their eyes were opened; they saw they were naked. The next thing that happens, God walks in the cool of the garden and says, "Where are you?" And man says, "I'm afraid because I'm naked, so I hid."

I don't think there is a culture anywhere where those three emotions are not universal: fear, sense of shame or inadequacy, and a desire to hide it. And when we think about happiness and why it is so elusive in our lives, it's okay to understand that there are ways in which we can feel better. But there are some fundamental sources and reasons for why it is elusive. It has something to do with the way this world is. To some extent, we may need to look at some of those spiritual roots for unhappiness and discontentment.

QUESTIONS FOR DISCUSSION

- *Compare Professor Frank's and Professor Lee's views on the origins of discontentment.*

- *How would you expect Professors Frank and Lee to differ in their theories of how unhappiness can be addressed?*

- *How do Professor Frank's comments on income and happiness bear on your thinking about salary and career?*

? For audience questions related to this topic, see page 40 *(As a believer, what is the motivation for happiness? And as an unbeliever, does a narrative of belief change how you think about happiness?)* and page 46 *(What's the difference between joy and happiness?).*

WORKING FOR MONEY?

Prof. Chignell: Nothing you're saying has anything to do with money. And yet you work in finance and you're an economist. You manage $350 billion. Why isn't money something that comes into the picture at least initially? And if it doesn't, why are you doing what you're doing professionally?

Prof. Lee: Somebody has to do it. *[Laughter]* The question of money is a good one. I think both Christians and non-Christians have a stigma around money. The concern is, on the one hand: If you're so smart, why aren't you rich? My area of research is on predicting stock returns. So the question we get is: "If you are so good at this, why aren't you rich?"

On the other hand the question is: "If you are so *good*, why are you rich?" If you look at the seven billion people who live on this planet, what justifies some people living so much better than other people?

I see myself as a creature. The most important thing is my reference to what my creator wanted. There is no success apart from that because I have to figure out why I'm made. So whether you manage money or are an educator, the real success is telling whether you are doing what you're called to do or what you feel you should do – and that you've done everything you can to try to understand that.

Some people think Christianity is about poverty or piety. I don't think the focus is on poverty but on priority. Think of things that God gives you as – in the eternal scheme of things – a bunch of zeros. But if you put God first, they become significant digits that potentially are useful. If you don't, they're still zeros.

Prof. Chignell: Both of you are now academics. Both of you could have gone on Wall Street and been fabulously wealthy. Say something about why you chose not to do that. Some people will think there's a kind of irrationality there.

A personal anecdote here: when I was in grad school at Yale, I would often be a TA for students who were heading in the Wall Street direction. They would be taking a philosophy class for whatever reason. And my fellow TA's and I got the impression they viewed us as smart but tragic cases, who got hung up on some question and couldn't get out of grad school. Why not just focus on making big money?

Prof. Frank: It's something that I feel in the business school is the most difficult message to communicate to students. They want to work for McKinsey or Goldman Sachs, they want to be a private equity person or a hedge fund manager, because they see the spectacularly big paychecks associated with those activities and they think that's the way to be happy. It's not the way to be happy. The evidence is very clear that salaries beyond a certain point really don't make much difference in the level of contentment people feel.

There's a concept in the psychological literature called "flow." When you're deeply immersed in an activity, the day or the hours fly by and you aren't even aware of it. Those are, for me, the very happiest days I ever experienced. When I'm writing a book, the first thing I want to do in the morning is just get to it. And I'm just carried along by the narrative, wanting it to progress. And so I'm not much of a companion when I'm experiencing flow. So I don't write books most of the time. But it's a joyous experience. And I know many other people have that experience in their work; but if what you want is to get rich, it will just be a matter of pure chance that you experience the joy of that flow.

The very most important thing to do when you pick a job is to pick a job that you think you have the capacity to love just for its own sake – never mind the salary. We know that salary is related to job characteristics. If you're going to do a morally compromised job, for example, you can get paid extra. If you write ad copy for RJR to try and convince teenagers to start smoking, you'll get paid three times as much as if you had the same skills and were writing copy for the American Cancer Society to try to persuade teenagers not to start smoking. The moral taint of the first job commands a premium. Just as Adam Smith said: nobody would be a garbage man unless there was a premium pay. Why should you work in those smelly conditions? I'd rather be a lifeguard.

The jobs that entail moral compromise pay most. If you think you want to make money, you ought to find the most morally culpable job or the most unpleasant conditions, because that'll be the one that pays the most. The absurdity of that strategy for choosing a job becomes clear if you play it out.

If you pick a job you love, you're going to get immersed in it; you're going to get good at it. And in the modern labor market, if you're the best at what you do, that's when material success comes your way. If you don't like what you do, what are the odds that you'll be the best at what you do? It could happen. But if you're a betting person you have to bet against that outcome.

So pick a place where people aren't doing things you'd be ashamed to do, because if you go there, you'll end up doing those things too. You don't behave differently from your environment for long. And pick a job where you'll just want to be doing that job and then you'll get good at it and the money will probably take care of itself. And if the money doesn't take care of itself, at least you'll be doing something you really like. If you focus only on the need to make income, you'll point yourself in the dead wrong direction.

Professor Lee: I don't disagree with Bob. But the way I think about it is: if you're a creature, your reference point is God. I'm not sure if getting paid more or less brings you closer or further away from that calling. I managed a portfolio for a not-for-profit Christian organization for ten years and we had very good returns. Is that a more spiritual endeavor than managing a lot of money for high-net-worth individuals? The calling is the calling. Price itself does not inform, if I'm clear about the calling.

It happens in every circle. In Christian circles, people may say, "Why are you an accounting professor? Why aren't you a pastor?" In our currency, that might be a more noble calling. But if that's not my calling, that's not a very spiritual thing. At the end of the day, it's between you and your Maker. Everybody else provides you input, but you make that decision in the context of your conscience before who you think created you and has a claim on your life.

Professor Chignell: Maybe you at least differ in this way. You think someone might be called to do something which isn't going to produce flow, a lot of joy or well-being.

Professor Lee: I totally resonate with this flow thing. As an example, it took my son a long time to commit his life to being a Christian. He was afraid that God was going to send him out of his flow. He was going to have to be an accountant or something.

It's very natural. If you don't have a spiritual orientation, it can be very uncomfortable having to ask someone for permission in your life. But if you think about who it is that you are trusting and if this is really the Creator, it's not like asking permission from your thesis advisor. This God potentially knows you and wants you to be in your flow; after all, he designed the flow. So it may not be a terrible thing.

QUESTIONS FOR DISCUSSION

- *For both presenters, success is connected to purpose. If you're made to "pass your stuff to the next round," success looks one way; if you're made to "please a creator," success looks another. What do you think is the central project or work of being human?*

- *To what extent does "flow" factor into your academic or career choices? Professor Frank mentioned that when he's in the flow of writing, he's not a good companion. What might be some particular tradeoffs or risks of pursuing a life of flow?*

? For audience questions related to this topic, see page 44 (*How do you reconcile your views on money with the Bible saying that the rich are not able to get into heaven?*) and page 45 (*Would you recommend people pursue a career in finance?*).

QUESTION AND ANSWER

SUCCESS

Summary of Questions from the Audience

- As an atheist, how do I deal with the emptiness I feel in pursuing virtue as a means to harmony for the group? (Answer on page 35)

- If we're being good because God is watching, are we really being good out of fear? Or is there something else? (Answer on page 36)

- By what metric do you measure virtue if not a religious one? (Answer on page 37)

- Should morality be integrated into our university system? (Answer on page 38)

- As a believer, what is the motivation for happiness? And as an unbeliever, does a narrative of belief change how you think about happiness? (Answer on page 40)

- Why do we see altruism in the human species but not in others? (Answer on page 43)

- How do you reconcile your views on money with the Bible saying that the rich are not able to get into heaven? (Answer on page 50)

- Would you recommend people pursue a career in finance? (Answer on page 45)

- What is the difference between joy and happiness? (Answer on page 46)

Question and Answer Session

Audience member: I see the pursuit of virtue as a means to achieve the harmony of the group, which will in turn be to my own benefit. Humans are gregarious by nature, so this is alright. However, as an atheist, I can't help feeling emptiness and some lack of purpose when I acknowledge this view. How do I deal with this – the emptiness, the lack of purpose?

Prof. Frank: I think as an empirical matter, atheists don't suffer disproportionately from emptiness or lack of purpose. The people who feel empty are those who don't have engaged relationships with friends, family and professional associates. There is nothing about how we came to have a desire for such relationships or a tendency to take satisfaction from having them that depends on how those came to be. Those are contingent facts about human beings that are clear however you think they arose.

If you feel empty or you feel you don't have anybody you think would return the envelope with $10,000 in it, in both those cases you need to get out more. Form relationships with people of a more lasting sort. If you're not able to form effective, engaging relationships with other people, then you're not an effective member of a team. If you're not an effective member of a team, then you probably won't enjoy much material success.

The human condition, on average, requires you to be a trustworthy, likable, loyal, honest member of a team. It may mean that you need to reach out more and dig a little deeper in your attempts to forge those relationships. People who report that they have a lot of close relationships consistently have greater life satisfaction.

Audience member: If we're being good because God is watching, are we really being good out of fear? Or is there something else?

Prof. Lee: I'm hoping that I don't feel I'm being good because there's an exam or because God is watching. I'm hoping that I being good because I want good, because I love good, because good is intrinsically valuable to me.

So how does one get that way? I'm not sure. I don't know. I think that there is a longing that is deeper than the longing for friendship or the longing for belonging, the longing for a sense of security. I think there's a longing for home – spiritually. We were made for fellowship with God and in the absence of that there is always a longing. We may not think there is an answer to that. As C.S. Lewis said, the fact that I feel hunger may not mean that I can find food, but it might show that there is such a thing as food. There is something deeper, a deeper desire in the human soul for a connection with a creator God.

Audience member: By what metric do you measure virtue if not religious belief? In a moral quandary, how can we gauge what actions are best?

Prof. Frank: As an economist, my natural inclination is to side with the people who measure the costs and benefits of the different alternatives and try to assign value to them as clearly and consistently as possible. And then when there's a tough call to make, try to make the choice that entails the greatest balance of goodness over harm.

I appreciate the idea that there are good reasons not to trust a consequentialist. Every interesting moral choice is one when you don't know if it's okay to do it because it may be harmful to others. If you're the one making the call, you have to estimate how beneficial it will be to you and how much harm it will cause to others. Those estimates are always ambiguous. Since you have an interest in the matter, you're liable to find yourself fudging upwards the benefits you'll get from the thing you want to do and playing down the harm it will cause to others. And you're more likely to do it than you ought to be in some cases. And as more and more people chose that way, norms fall apart and there's a race to the bottom.

I think, in principle, the way to resolve them most satisfactorily is to look for the values at stake on the competing sides and try to assess them. And if the total balance of gain vs. harm is bigger for one choice than the other, then it's always possible to divide up the gains so that everybody comes out better off. And when you can make people come out ahead in a win-win sense, then you should and you're more likely to get a good outcome.

Audience member: Dr. Lee asked, "Do we need more smart people or more good people?" in reference to the manner in which our university system is organized. Is this to imply that faith should be integrated in our school and university systems?

Prof. Lee: I think Cornell is a leading force in separating the two, so I'm not that retro. But I think it's been healthy both for the spiritual pursuit and the educational to think carefully about what each one is about.

We relegate all discussions of everything religious to dorm rooms and beer parlors. There was a time when university meant 'universal, but in diversity' and we talked not only about knowledge but also about wisdom: the ability to apply technical knowledge in your day-to-day living, integrated across many fields. And that's a healthy thing. I think we should talk about what is important, what's valuable, what it would look like, why is it that at certain cost, your harm means more to me than my benefit. A lot of these things are worth debating.

Even more important, we need to recognize that faith and reason are not polar opposites. I have one fishing buddy who is a very intelligent economist who once told me: "Faith means you cannot question it. If you question it, then it's axiomatically no longer faith." I think that's just not true. Life is all about how you decide under uncertainty. And for the most important things in your life, you will always be deciding under uncertainty. I can't mathematically prove the plane that took me to Boston would get me there safely, but I bet my life on it. I can't mathematically prove that my wife of 30 years loves me, but I bet my life on it.

In the moral and relational domains of your life, you're constantly making those decisions. In those decisions, you're making a weight-of-evidence type assessment. Somehow in academics, we start to think if it isn't in the realm of matter, energy, something that's material, that somehow we would be encroaching, and I don't think that's a good thing. I think it's worth talking about the role of uncertainty in moral settings and how we can live better. I think universities are supposed to be about that.

Prof. Chignell: It sounds like you agree about the behaviors and some of the results – happiness, joy, flow – but that it's a disagreement about the way to *motivate* the behaviors. Or the underlying narrative, the worldview, by which you would tell the story. Why are you doing what you're dong? Why do you think it's getting you to where you're supposed to be going? Charles, you're going to tell it in a religious fashion and appeal to God's will and vocation. Bob, you'll have a different kind of story that's more naturalistic, referencing Darwinian and consequentialist theories. But it doesn't look as if the results – practically, behaviorally – are that different.

Prof. Lee: I'm not sure that they are all that different. I'm not sure whether you can say empirically that people lived better, more moral lives because they adhere to one view or another. But one observation about this whole process of faith is that God doesn't coerce faith. In other words, if you say to God: "Why don't you prove yourself? And I will believe in you. I'm in a good mood and I'll give you thirty seconds." God often doesn't engage in that sort of thing. He doesn't entertain it. If God wants to arm wrestle you with physical evidence – if you believe in him, you'll have a better life – boom, there's no game, it's over. Because if he wants to coerce you through physical evidence, he could.

I like what Blaise Pascal, the mathematician, said. He was a philosopher in his spare time. What Blaise Pascal said is that the ultimate end of reason is to show you that reason alone is not enough. If you follow the rationality of your brain to the top, you'll realize that's where the road ends. The rational being recognizes there are limitations to his rationality. And then he looks up and sees a billion stars in the night sky and looks down and sees a rocket sitting there. And he recognizes that the rational thing, if he wants to reach the skies, is to leave his road and get on that rocket. That's a rational conclusion.

And another thing Pascal said was that there is always sufficient evidence for those whose inclination is to seek God. There's also sufficient evidence for those whose inclination is to do otherwise.

That's a reasonable design for a God who does not want to coerce. If we all had certainty all the time, we'd all make the same decisions. Where we make different decisions is how we weigh the uncertainty. In matters of faith, that's all-important.

Prof. Chignell: Robert, I found an op-ed you wrote in *USA Today*: "No good comes from arguing about religion. Look at the Middle East and the Republican Primary." But I do want you to argue a little bit about religion. That is to say, does having the narrative that Charles is putting forward change anything with respect to how you think about happiness and do you want to reject any part of what it changes?

Prof. Frank: My mother was a very spiritual person. She was deeply involved in Indonesian meditation in the last decades of her life. They would seek the will of God, was the way she put it. She used to worry about me that I didn't have a spiritual connection of anything like the one she had. And I could see what it did for her: she was a charismatic woman, you could sense there was this aura about her. I lack that, I feel. I don't have that quality that she had.

It seemed to be good to have that quality. Where can I get some of that? "Just be religious and you'll get it." But I didn't think that was an option for me.

I once spent a week with the Dalai Lama in India. A group of us went to talk with him about what Western scholars had written about why you should be moral if you aren't religious. It becomes instantly apparent when you're in the same space as him that there is some radiant spiritual quality that he has that I don't have. I don't know many people who have anything remotely like that. I think it would be great to have some of that. But I don't see what path for me is accessible to go there. I would have to give up other things that are an important part of who I am. I'm not unhappy enough with who I am to be willing to do that.

Prof. Chignell: Is it believing things you think are false?

Prof. Frank: I wouldn't presume to say they're false. It's to believe things I can't find compelling reason to believe.

Prof. Lee: Nobody wants to believe in what they find no compelling reason to believe. There are times when you may need a little help to have illumination. If God's light is like light coming in and there is a big curtain there and you can't see it, you may need help to have it removed. It is a reasonable and rational thing: if God is bigger than you, and you'll have a problem lifting that curtain, it's reasonable to ask him.

Audience member: If having emotions and doing good benefits the individual, why didn't that same trait evolve in other animals? In other words, why do we see extremes of altruism and virtue in the human species and not in others?

Prof. Frank: Frans de Waal who is a noted primatologist and a dear friend of mine, has written several quite compellingly good books suggesting we do see the origins of these traits in humans in other primates. Still the differences are striking. The three-year-old child immediately knows what the adult is trying to do and rushes over to help, even if it's an unrelated adult. The chimpanzees don't seem to get that the adult is trying to do something, or show any inclination to help. The idea of giving up something of your own and getting a benefit later or maybe not at all is a very difficult problem to solve. You need emotional capacities and deep communication skills to express emotions in ways that others can decipher and then make predictions about what you do. Those are difficult and complicated problems to solve. It looks like other species are at an early stage of solving these problems but haven't gotten nearly as far as humans have.

Audience member: How do you reconcile your views on money with the Bible saying that the rich are not able to get into heaven?

Prof. Lee: I'm glad you're reading the Bible. Jesus *does* say it is harder for the rich to get into heaven than for a camel to get through the eye of a needle. That passage has two examples around it. The first is a rich young man whom Jesus tells to "go sell everything and follow me" and he declines, and that precipitates this comment. Jesus looked at this young man and loved him and said, "It's sad. It's sad that those riches are more important to you than something else."

Then there's the story of a fat little guy named Zacchaeus, a wealthy tax collector – today's hedge fund manager. Jesus looks at this guy in the tree and says, "Come on down. I want to have dinner with you." And he says, "If I owe anyone anything, I will pay him back four times over." The thing that is really important is where your heart is, what's *really* important deep down. And that isn't for me to judge. You need to know.

Prof. Chignell: You'd agree that you cannot serve both God and money.

Prof. Lee: Yeah. But you can make money and serve others. What you do with one hand, don't let the other hand know. In other words, if you're generous, don't go around making a big deal about it.

Audience member: Would you recommend that people pursue a career in finance?

Prof. Lee: You need *good* hedge fund managers. You need good honest people. It's a scarcity.

Let me give you an example: I know one guy who worked for a hedge fund for two years. He didn't know that much before he started and then after two years started a company directly competing with these guys. He was asked why. And he said, "You know, I got $100 million seed money. How often do you get that?" In other words, he didn't disagree with the fact that this was not a moral thing to do. But he said, "Hey you'd understand, it's $100 million." Well, here's the tension. He wouldn't feel that way if someone did it to him. If you were in that situation, would you do it, too?

Here is the human dilemma: there is a standard higher than the sky, and if, in your deepest, most lucid moment you desire that standard that you can reach for, then you should reach for it; you shouldn't assume it cannot be reached.

Audience member: What's the difference between joy and happiness? Happiness seems to be based on circumstances, while joy seems to have a deeper meaning based on one's broader outlook on life.

Prof. Frank: I think the common understanding of those two terms is that they are different, and the difference is, in a way, similar to the difference between comfort and pleasure: pleasure being analogous to joy and comfort to happiness.

Comfort is the opposite of discomfort. If you're not hungry then you're comfortable. If you want to have pleasure, you have to be uncomfortable (hungry) first. The act of moving between states – from hungry to sated – is the moment of pleasure. Joy has a similar dynamic component to it, the dynamic state between a bad state and a good state. The exhilaration, the surprise, to be so much better than what just was. Satisfaction is a more muted concept from that.

Programming some joy into your life, you might do as some cultures did: fast for a while and then feast. There are ways to construct that experience. But there are many other practical things more worth worrying about than that.

If you want to lead a happy life, you'll have to ask: Will I have money enough to lead the kind of life I aspire to lead? In New York City, if you want to have a couple of kids and want to educate them well that means $35,000 a year tuition. Maybe it would be hard to lead the kind of life you want to live. Our kids walked three blocks to elementary school and went to school with kids from all around the world who lived right here.

If you choose your environment carefully – and it's different at different stages of your life – you can construct a life where you don't need lots of money to do the things that are *really* important to you. You can pick a task and try to get good at it, try to get immersed in it. And you can build your network of close people around you, both professionally and personally.

All these things are within reach for people, whether they are believers or not. There are good choices available. And I think when people think *only* about how I can succeed in a narrow material sense of the term, you're on the road to somewhere and then you get there and it wasn't anywhere.

Prof. Lee: I don't know how to compare across subjects. Let me give you a time-series observation about one subject: me. You may not like me much today. But I assure you, you would like me much less if I hadn't become a Christian many years ago.

I think of happiness as related to moods, up and down. I think of joy as some sort of quiet state that when I reflect upon reality, wellness swells up from nowhere.

Before I was a Christian, in my most lucid moments, in the quiet moments of my life, I was in retrospect not joyful. Melancholy. I seemed to see the world *too* much for what it was. The difference is that in my most lucid moments now that I am a Christian, I still have times when I go up and down. But when I see things most clearly, joy is not an unreasonable word to describe how I feel.

COMPLETE LIST OF
QUESTIONS FOR DISCUSSION

From *Two Views of Successful Living* **(page 9)**

- Can you sketch your basic worldview using the "security guard" questions: *Who are you? Why are you here? Where are you going?*

- How would you define success right now? Can you trace how your worldview shapes your particular vision of success?

- Professor Lee emphasizes the importance of virtue in human happiness. In your experience, how are the two related? Have you experienced one without the other?

- Given the quotation by David Foster Wallace, what are your "default settings"? Have you experienced – or seen others – being "eaten alive" by what they worship?

- How do you respond to Professor Lee's critique of privatized faith and a siloed university? What other models are there for education and morality?

From *Two Views of Successful Living Continued* **(page 16)**

- According to a Darwinian understanding, what makes humans unique? How does that square with your experience of being human?

- What are the elements of success, in Professor Frank's view?

- Professor Frank says that succeeding in being trusted is very simple: *"Just be that kind of person. If you're not that kind of person...there will be something different about you that will make people not quite comfortable trusting you."* Where do you think that lack of inner peace comes from? What is your experience in "just being that kind of person"?

- How are virtue and success related from a Darwinian point of view? How does that compare with Professor Lee's approach or your own answer on page 8?

- Professor Frank implies that emotions drive moral decisions. How do you respond to that? How do you adopt unaffected empathetic emotions?

From *Aiming for Character?* **(page 23)**

- Compare Professor Frank's and Professor Lee's views of the origins of virtue. Are they compatible?

- Given both professors' comments and your own experience, list all of the reasons for being virtuous. Which do you find most compelling? To what extent do any of those reasons enable you to be virtuous?

- Professor Lee draws a distinction between why we might strive for virtue, and how well we do at achieving it. Reflect on what he says about "minding the gap" in your own life.

From *Pursuing Happiness?* **(page 27)**

- Compare Professor Frank's and Professor Lee's views on the origins of discontentment.

- How would you expect Professors Frank and Lee to differ in their theories of how unhappiness can be addressed?

- How do Professor Frank's comments on income and happiness bear on your thinking about salary and career?

From *Working for Money?* **(page 32)**

- For both presenters, success is connected to purpose. If you're made to "pass your stuff to the next round," success looks one way; if you're made to "please a creator," success looks another. What do you think is the central project, purpose or work of being human?

- To what extent does "flow" factor into your academic or career choices? Professor Frank mentioned that when he's in the flow of writing, he's not a good companion. What might be some particular tradeoffs or risks for you of pursuing a life of flow?

ABOUT THE PRESENTERS

Charles M. C. Lee is the Joseph McDonald Professor of Accounting at the Graduate School of Business, Stanford University. He is also Co-Chair of the Accounting Department at the Guanghua School of Management, Peking University. Prior to joining Stanford, Dr. Lee was a Managing Director at Barclays Global Investors (BGI). Professor Lee received his Ph.D. from Cornell University and holds a Certificate in Biblical Studies from Ontario Theological Seminary.

Robert H. Frank is the Henrietta Johnson Louis Professor of Management and Professor of Economics at Johnson Graduate School of Management, Cornell University. He is also the co-director of the Paduano Seminar in business ethics at NYU's Stern School of Business. He received his B.S. in mathematics from Georgia Tech and his M.A. in statistics and Ph.D. in economics, both from the University of California at Berkeley.

Andrew Chignell is Associate Professor in Cornell's Susan Linn Sage School of Philosophy, with secondary appointments in German Studies and Religious Studies.

ABOUT THE VERITAS FORUM

The Veritas Forum hosts university events that engage students and faculty in discussions about life's hardest questions and the relevance of Jesus Christ to all of life.

Every year, hundreds of university community members host, plan and coordinate Veritas Forums on their local campuses, with guidance from national and regional staff across North America, Europe and Asia.

We seek to inspire the shapers of tomorrow's culture to connect their hardest questions with the person and story of Jesus Christ.

For more information about The Veritas Forum, including recordings and upcoming events, visit www.veritas.org.

15670979R00039